THE SHOSHONES

BY LIZ SONNEBORN

CONSULTANTS:
JOHN WASHAKIE
EASTERN SHOSHONE, B.A., HISTORY, UNIVERSITY OF WYOMING

AND GLENDA TROSPER
DIRECTOR OF THE EASTERN SHOSHONE TRIBAL CULTURAL CENTER,
FORT WASHAKIE, WYOMING

LERNER PUBLICATIONS COMPANY
MINNEAPOLIS

ABOUT THE COVER IMAGE: The Shoshone people are known for their beautiful beadwork. This pair of beaded moccasins features a pattern of the Shoshone rose.

PHOTO ACKNOWLEDGMENTS:

The photos in this book are used courtesy of: © 2006 Harvard University, Peabody Museum Photo, 35-78-10/5011 N31509, pp. 1, 3, 4, 16, 24, 36; © Laura Westlund/Independent Picture Service, p. 5; © Luther Linkhart/SuperStock, p. 6; © Marilyn "Angel" Wynn/Nativestock.com, pp. 7, 8, 10, 11, 13, 14, 15, 17, 19, 25, 32, 35, 39, 40, 42, 44, 50; © Kennan Ward/CORBIS, p. 9; © Theo Allofs/zefa/CORBIS, p. 12; © Ray Bial, pp. 18, 37, 41, 43, 46, 49; © North Wind Picture Archives, p. 20; Library of Congress, pp. 21 (LC-USZ62-50631), 28 (LC-USZC4-2343); © Hulton Archive/Getty Images, p. 23; Denver Public Library, Western History Collection, p. 26; © Bettmann/CORBIS, p. 27; © Kevin R. Morris/CORBIS, p. 29; Idaho State Historical Society (75-14.1), p. 30; © CORBIS, pp. 31, 34, 38; American Portraits/Courtesy Mercaldo Archives, p. 33; © Peter Essick/Aurora/Getty Images, p. 47; © Ilka Hartmann, p. 48.

Front Cover: Collection of the Jackson Hole Historical Society and Museum, 1991.0087.032.

Lerner Publications Company
A division of Lerner Publishing Group
241 First Avenue North
Minneapolis, MN 55401 U.S.A.

Website address: www.lernerbooks.com

Library of Congress Cataloging-in-Publication Data

Sonneborn, Liz.
    The Shoshones / by Liz Sonneborn.
      p.   cm. — (Native American histories)
    Includes bibliographical references and index.
    ISBN-13: 978-0-8225-2849-4 (lib. bdg. : alk. paper)
    ISBN-10: 0-8225-2849-5 (lib. bdg. : alk. paper)
      1. Shoshoni Indians—History—Juvenile literature. 2. Shoshoni Indians—Social life and customs—Juvenile literature. I. Title. II. Series.
    E99.S4S65   2007
    978.004'974574—dc22   2005005652

Manufactured in the United States of America
1 2 3 4 5 6 – DP – 12 11 10 09 08 07

CONTENTS

CHAPTER 1

THE SHOSHONE WAY

WHEN THE EARTH WAS STILL YOUNG, two women gave Coyote a lidded basket as he set off on a journey. They warned him not to open it. But Coyote was curious to see what was inside. From time to time, he peeked under the lid. Each time, a few human beings crawled out. Soon, small groups of humans lived all over Pia Sokopia, the homeland of the Shoshone people.

The Western Shoshone Indian tribe has long told the story of Coyote and his basket. This is one tale the Shoshones tell of how they came to live in their large territory. The Shoshone homeland originally included land in what would later become California, Nevada, Utah, Idaho, Wyoming, and Montana.

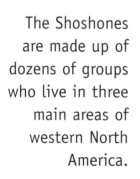

The Shoshones are made up of dozens of groups who live in three main areas of western North America.

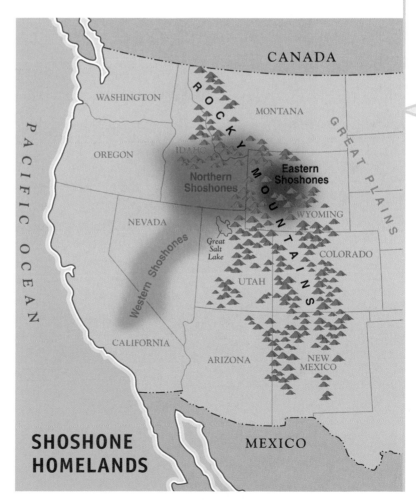

SHOSHONE HOMELANDS

THE WESTERN SHOSHONES

The land in the southwestern part of Shoshone territory was dry and rough. Few animals or plants could live there. The tribe members living in this region became known as the Western Shoshones. For them, just staying alive was hard.

The Western Shoshones' land was not rich enough to farm. Instead, they searched for wild plants and hunted animals for food. Each season, the Western Shoshones moved wherever these foods were most plentiful. Usually, they traveled in small groups made up of just a few families.

Sagebrush and mountains cover the southwestern part of Shoshone territory.

Shoshone women placed the plants they gathered in baskets like this one. They carried the baskets on their backs.

Women and children gathered nuts, seeds, and berries. They carried these foods in tightly woven baskets made of willow and other plants. Women rubbed resin into some baskets. Resin is a liquid that seeps from tree trunks. When the resin dried, the baskets could hold water.

Pine nuts grow inside pinecones on piñon trees. Pine nuts are an important traditional food for Western Shoshones.

In the fall, the Western Shoshones collected their most important plant food—pine nuts. These are the seeds of the piñon tree. If the Shoshone women worked hard, they could gather enough pine nuts to feed their families through the winter. Shoshone women ground the nuts into tiny pieces. They added water to the ground nuts to make a tasty mush that could be served hot or cold.

Western Shoshone men hunted to add to the food supply. They tracked and killed some large animals, such as bighorn sheep, antelope, and deer. But more often, the only animals the men could find were squirrels, rabbits, and birds. In the southern parts of Shoshone territory, hunters had to settle for lizards and grasshoppers.

Sometimes Western Shoshones ate large animals, such as the desert bighorn sheep.

Winters were often difficult for the Western Shoshones. If they were unable to find and store enough food, they could go hungry. To stay warm, the Western Shoshones built huts. The huts were made from wooden frames covered with bark or earth. Sometimes a family built a fire inside the hut. A hole in the roof allowed the smoke to escape. The Shoshones also kept warm by huddling under blankets made from dozens of rabbit skins sewn together.

In the mountains, Western Shoshones used brush to build winter huts.

Shoshones in the North picked chokecherries and dug up
bitterroots and camas bulbs. They boiled or steamed
the roots and bulbs before eating them.

THE NORTHERN SHOSHONES

Life was not as hard for the Northern Shoshones
of present-day Idaho. It was easier to find food in
their territory. Much of their land was covered
with wild plants they could cook and eat. The
camas root was a particular favorite. Women dug
up these roots using pointed sticks.

There was plenty of salmon in the rivers
of Northern Shoshone territory.

Waterways filled with fish also kept the
Northern Shoshones well fed. Using nets, traps,
and spears, men fished for trout and perch in
streams. In the spring, rivers were full of salmon.
For many months, Northern Shoshone families
feasted on fresh and dried fish.

Northern Shoshone men hunted other animals too. Hunters set out on their own or in groups to search for deer, elk, and sheep. Sometimes they crept up on antelope, wearing an antelope skin as a disguise. Animal skins and fur also made warm winter clothing.

Sometimes Shoshone hunters would cover themselves with animal skins, such as deerskin, to sneak up on their prey.

THE SPIRIT WORLD

The Shoshones believed that spirits took the form of plants and animals. These powerful spirits could protect human beings from harm or illness. The Shoshones often tried to gain power from these spirits. For the Western Shoshones, one way was the vision quest. During a vision quest, a young man headed off alone to a faraway spot. For days, he went without food and water while waiting for a vision of a spirit. If the young man saw a spirit, it protected him for life.

Shoshones often left behind drawings of the visions they saw. This symbol was carved on Legend Rock in Woming.

Costumed dancers perform the Grass Dance. The fringes on their costumes symbolize prairie grass swaying in the wind. Early Shoshones held the Grass Dance each spring as their people prayed for rain and good crops.

The Shoshones also performed ceremonies to communicate with the spirit world. The most common among the Western Shoshones was the Round Dance. Often, a Round Dance was held after the pine nut harvest or a successful rabbit hunt. During this ceremony, everyone linked arms and moved in a circle while singers sang special songs. Through dancing and singing, the Shoshones asked the spirits to make their world safe.

CHAPTER 2

A CHANGING WORLD

FOR HUNDREDS OF YEARS, the Shoshones traded with other Native American tribes. The Shoshones offered them finely woven baskets. In exchange, the American Indian traders gave the Shoshones treasures from faraway places. The Shoshones got shells from the Pacific Ocean. They got buffalo skins from the Great Plains, a large grassy area to the east.

In the early 1700s, the Shoshones' trading partners started offering them new trade goods, including horses. American Indian traders got most of these items from Spanish soldiers and settlers living to the southeast of Shoshone territory. Spaniards had begun coming to the area in the 1500s to explore and set up missions.

LIFE WITH HORSES

The Shoshones had never seen horses before. But they immediately knew how valuable these animals were. Horses allowed them to travel farther and faster. Horses became particularly valuable to the Northern and Eastern Shoshones.

Horses quickly became part of Shoshone life.

Since about 1500, a branch of the Shoshones lived in present-day Wyoming. They were the Eastern Shoshones. Once the Eastern and Northern Shoshones had horses, some of them began hunting buffalo on the Great Plains. They adopted many customs of Plains Indians. They started living in tipis. These cone-shaped houses were covered with buffalo hides and could be packed and carried easily.

Eastern and Northern Shoshones lived in tipis like this.

This buffalo-hide shield shows a Shoshone warrior on horseback battling a Crow enemy.

The Eastern and Northern Shoshones also began looking to powerful leaders to organize buffalo hunts and to fight other American Indians for control of hunting grounds. However, some of their northern neighbors, such as the Blackfeet and the Crow, had horses and guns, which they got from French fur traders. The Shoshones' enemies began riding into Shoshone territory and taking over their best lands.

Horses were far less useful to the Western Shoshones. Their territory had little water and grassland to feed these animals. Without horses or guns, the Western Shoshones could not easily protect themselves. Ute Indians raided Western Shoshone villages to kidnap women and children. The raiders often sold Shoshone captives to the Spanish explorers in the area. The Spanish forced the American Indians to be slaves and do work they did not want to do themselves.

Spanish conquerors forced the Shoshones to become their slaves. Here, Native Americans are made to carry Spanish gear.

Many Native American peoples, such as the Shoshones, helped Lewis and Clark on their journey to the Pacific Ocean.

LEWIS AND CLARK

In 1805, another group came to Shoshone territory. They were explorers led by Meriwether Lewis and William Clark. President Thomas Jefferson had sent them to explore lands in the western United States.

Lewis and Clark were traveling with Sacagawea, a young Shoshone woman. The explorers did not know the Shoshone language, so Sacagawea spoke for them. She made it clear that the explorers came in peace. Sacagawea also asked the Shoshones for help in getting across the great Rocky Mountains.

SACAGAWEA (ca. 1788–1812 or 1884) was kidnapped by Hidatsa Indians when she was ten years old. After five years, they sold her to Toussaint Charbonneau, a French Canadian fur trader.

In 1804, Charbonneau and Sacagawea met explorers Lewis and Clark. The explorers hired Charbonneau as a translator. Sacagawea joined them on their trip west. The journey was difficult. But Sacagawea made it easier. She collected roots to eat. She also helped guide the explorers to Shoshone territory.

Near the Rocky Mountains, the explorers met with a Shoshone leader named Cameahwait. They asked Sacagawea along to translate. When she saw Cameahwait, she shouted with joy. Cameahwait was her brother, whom she had not seen for years. Cameahwait happily gave the explorers fresh horses and helped them cross the Rocky Mountains.

What happened to Sacagawea after her travels with Lewis and Clark is unclear. Some say she died of disease in 1812. But many Shoshones believe she returned to her homeland and lived there until 1884.

Sacagawea is one of the most famous American Indian women in history.

Lewis and Clark soon left the Shoshones' lands and continued west. Their travels proved to be a great success. They wrote down everything they saw and made some of the first maps of the American West. Lewis and Clark's short visit did not have much effect on the Shoshones. But their writings made many Americans want to go to western lands, including the Shoshones' homeland.

CHAPTER 3
LOSING GROUND

THE EXPLORERS OF THE LEWIS AND CLARK EXPEDITION were the first whites to arrive in the heart of Shoshone territory. But they were far from the last. Soon, other explorers and fur traders began traveling through Shoshone lands.

Some white travelers angered the Shoshones. They killed animals that Shoshone hunters needed to feed their own families. But for the most part, the Shoshones got along with the newcomers, particularly the traders. In the summers, the tribe began attending yearly gatherings called rendezvous. These were great parties where western American Indians and whites met to trade.

American Indians and white traders met each summer between 1825 and 1840 at Fort Bridger in Wyoming to trade beaver pelts and other goods.

By about 1840, traders stopped coming to Shoshone territory. Beaver fur went out of fashion in Europe, ending the fur trade. Soon, other whites began heading west. They were settlers bound for the rich farmland in the area of modern-day Oregon and California. The only way to get there was to follow trails that cut through Shoshone territory.

A wagon train of settlers crosses a steep pass through the Rocky Mountains. Thousands of settlers traveled through Shoshone lands on their way west.

A family of Mormon settlers stands outside their mud and log home in Utah.

Soon, thousands of settlers were driving covered wagons through the tribe's homelands. These newcomers killed many of the animals hunted by the Shoshones. They also spread diseases, such as smallpox, that killed many tribe members. Members of the Mormon Church also began settling on Shoshone land in present-day Utah in 1847.

This image shows mining in the Comstock Lode.
Large amounts of gold and silver were found
in Nevada in the 1850s.

The next year, gold was found in California. A wave of miners rushed west, further taking over Shoshone lands. Even more people came after silver was discovered at Comstock Lode in present-day Nevada. To make mineshafts and houses, the silver miners cut down forests of piñon trees. Many Shoshones went hungry because they could not collect enough pine nuts to survive.

BATTLING OUTSIDERS

By the 1860s, the Shoshones were desperate and angry. They were tired of seeing outsiders take over and destroy their lands. Eastern Shoshones attacked Crow Indians who were moving onto their lands. The Northern Shoshones and Bannock Indians started striking back at white settlers. They raided white settlements and stole cattle and horses. They attacked wagon trains and stagecoaches traveling through their lands.

Crowheart Butte, Wyoming, was the site of a major battle between the Shoshones and Crow Indians in 1866. The two groups fought over hunting grounds.

To punish the Shoshone raiders, U.S. Army colonel Patrick Edward Connor and his troops attacked a Northern Shoshone camp in 1863. They killed about 250 Shoshone men, women, and children.

POCATELLO (c. 1815–1884) was an important leader of the Northern Shoshones in the late 1800s. As he rose to power, more and more whites were arriving in Shoshone territory. Pocatello's followers were often blamed for attacks on settlers traveling on western trails. In 1859, the U.S. Army captured him. Pocatello and his people later settled on the Fort Hall Indian Reservation in Idaho. The city of Pocatello, Idaho, is named for him.

This image shows a government army camp at Fort Bridger in southwestern Wyoming. Soldiers patrolled the area and protected settlers and travelers from American Indian raids.

The U.S. government wanted to end the Shoshone attacks once and for all. It sent officials to make treaties with the Shoshones. In these agreements, the United States promised to set aside lands for many Shoshone bands. These areas of land were called reservations. Included in the treaties was another pledge by the United States. It would make sure whites and other American Indians stayed outside the reservations' borders.

A Shoshone family sits in a tipi on the Fort Hall reservation.

RESERVATION LIFE

The United States, however, did not always keep its promises. The Northern Shoshones and their Bannock Indian neighbors were sent to the Fort Hall reservation in present-day Idaho in 1867. But within a few years, white settlers moved onto some of the reservation's best land. U.S. officials did nothing to stop them. Little by little, the United States chipped away at the size of Fort Hall by changing the reservation borders.

In 1868, the Eastern Shoshones were granted land along the Wind River in present-day Wyoming. Led by Chief Washakie, the Wind River Shoshones were fairly friendly with settlers. Some of Washakie's followers even fought on the side of the U.S. Army in a campaign against the Sioux and other Plains Indians in the 1870s.

WASHAKIE (c. 1804–1900) was a leader of the Eastern Shoshones for decades. He grew up among the Northern Shoshones of present-day Idaho. As an adult, he joined a buffalo-hunting band to the east. Though a great warrior, Washakie chose to make peace with whites. He negotiated the treaty that created the Wind River Indian Reservation in what is now Wyoming. Washakie remained the reservation's most powerful leader until his death.

In 1878, the Eastern Shoshones also had trouble with their reservation. The United States sent nearly one thousand Arapaho Indians to Wind River. The Eastern Shoshones felt betrayed. They did not want to share their reservation with anyone, but especially not with the Arapaho, one of their traditional enemies. Washakie met with U.S. officials. He insisted they move the Arapaho off the Wind River reservation, but they ignored the Shoshone leader's demands.

Shoshones gather for a meeting at Fort Washakie, Wyoming, in 1892. Chief Washakie is on the far left, standing and pointing.

In the late 1800s, Jack Tendoy *(right)* and other Lemhi Shoshones fought to remain on the land set aside for their people near the Salmon River in Idaho.

The end of the 1800s was a difficult period for the Shoshones. During this time, they lost most of their territory to the U.S. government. On reservations, they also lost their freedom. However, after centuries in their harsh surroundings, the Shoshones were familiar with hardship. They were survivors, ready and willing to build a new life.

CHAPTER 4
INTO THE FUTURE

DURING THE EARLY 1900s, the Shoshones on reservations struggled. They were very poor. The U.S. government provided them with small amounts of food called rations. But the rations were barely enough to keep them alive. They were also pressured to give away more of their land.

To deal with their troubles, many Shoshones turned to American Indian religions. For instance, the Shoshones at Wind River and Fort Hall began performing the Sun Dance. Plains Indians introduced them to this ceremony. The Shoshones believe that performing the Sun Dance keeps their people healthy and strong.

In the 1930s, the United States let American Indian groups form their own governments. Shoshone governments managed money the Shoshones got from farming and renting pastureland.

Cows graze on pastureland on the Shoshone-Bannock reservation at Fort Hall in Idaho.

In time, Shoshone governments helped establish businesses owned and run by the Shoshones. They also used funds from the U.S. government to build houses and provide health care for the Shoshone people. These changes improved the Shoshones' lives, and their population grew. In 2000, about 12,000 Americans claimed to be at least part Shoshone.

A classroom on the Wind River Indian Reservation in Wyoming in 1939 had white and American Indian students.

A group of Eastern Shoshone boys plays basketball on the Wind River Indian Reservation in Wyoming.

MODERN SHOSHONE LIFE

Many Shoshones live on reservations created in the 1800s. Most Eastern Shoshones still make their home on the Wind River Indian Reservation in Wyoming. Many Northern Shoshones live on Idaho's Fort Hall Indian Reservation, which they share with the Bannock Indians. The people of that reservation call themselves the Shoshone-Bannock Tribes—or the Sho-Ban, for short.

The Edmo family spends time together at their home on the Fort Hall Indian Reservation.

The Northern Shoshones also include the Lemhi Shoshones, the Boise Shoshones, and the Northwestern Shoshones. They live in parts of Montana, Idaho, and Utah.

The Western Shoshones are more scattered. They live in communities and on a few small reservations in Nevada, Utah, California, and Idaho. One group of Western Shoshones has two reservations near the border of Utah and Nevada. This group is known as the Goshute tribe.

No matter where they live, the Shoshones face similar challenges. Their most pressing problem is still poverty. Many Shoshones are poor and unemployed. Some live in broken-down houses. Some do not have any health care and suffer from serious diseases, such as diabetes.

Many poor Shoshones look to elected tribal councils for help. Members of tribal councils make important decisions for people on their reservations.

This building houses tribal offices on the Shoshone-Bannock reservation at Fort Hall.

The Sho-Ban are governed by the Fort Hall
Business Council. It was founded in the 1930s and
has seven elected members. The Shoshone
Business Council leads the Shoshones of the
Wind River reservation. The Arapaho on Wind
River have their own council. It often meets with
the Shoshones' council members to discuss
matters that affect the entire reservation.

An Arapaho and Shoshone Indian council is pictured
at Fort Washakie in the early 1900s.

Single-story homes at Fort Hall, Idaho, provide housing for many of the reservation's families.

The Shoshone tribal councils help decide what to do with money the Shoshones receive from the U.S. government. Much of this money is spent to improve the housing, health care, and schools on their reservations. The councils also make deals with companies interested in using the natural resources on reservation land. For instance, Wind River has supplies of oil and natural gas.

Shoshone rancher Larry Teton ropes cattle
during a fall roundup at his ranch on
the Fort Hall Indian Reservation.

The Shoshones' reservation governments also
operate businesses. For instance, the Sho-Ban run
a trading post, clothing store, restaurant, gas
station, and casino. These businesses bring money
to the community. They also provide much-
needed jobs for people on the reservation. Other
industries that employ Shoshones include farming
and ranching.

Modern Shoshones live much as other Americans do. They wear the same clothes, eat the same foods, and live in the same types of houses. But some Shoshone ways remain. Most Shoshones speak English at home, but children continue to learn the Shoshone language in reservation schools. Several Shoshone groups also continue to make and sell baskets and other traditional crafts.

JACK MALOTTE (b. 1953) is a Western Shoshone artist. His artwork explores how modern American Indian people live. While studying at the California College of Arts and Crafts, Malotte worked as a firefighter. His work in forests inspired him to draw and paint beautiful landscapes. Since 1981, he has been a full-time artist. His art uses humor to show how American Indians join old and new ways.

COMING TOGETHER

The Shoshones still gather for ceremonies. The residents of Fort Hall and Wind River hold yearly summer festivals. The festivals give the Shoshones a chance to visit with relatives who have moved off the reservation. Over several days, Shoshones from all over the West celebrate their roots by dancing, singing, and playing games.

A Shoshone dancer wearing traditional dress dances at the annual Shoshone-Bannock Indian Festival. The festival is the one of the largest powwows in North America.

Yucca Mountain in Nevada is known as Snake Mountain to the Western Shoshones. They gather at this sacred place to perform religious ceremonies.

In recent years, many Shoshones from different bands and reservations have also come together to protect their rights. Some have protested the U.S. government's attempts to cut down their remaining piñon forests. Others have fought to protect sacred Shoshone sites. One site is Nevada's Yucca Mountain. The Shoshones want to keep the U.S. government from dumping nuclear waste there.

MARY AND CARRIE DANN

For more than thirty years, Western Shoshone sisters Mary and Carrie Dann have fought to make the United States keep its treaty promises. In 1863, the Treaty of Ruby Valley granted the Western Shoshones a huge piece of land in present-day Nevada. In the late 1800s, white settlers took over most of this territory. The Danns say that Western Shoshones still own this land. The Danns refuse to stop grazing their horses there, even though the U.S. government has ordered them to pay high fines. In April 2005, Mary Dann died in a ranch accident. The Danns' struggle for justice, however, still inspires American Indians throughout the country.

Carrie and Mary Dann *(second and third from the right)* and other leaders of the Western Shoshone Sacred Lands Association pose for a photo in 1979.

The Shoshones have also fought the United States in court. They claim that the U.S. government illegally took control of lands given to the Shoshones in treaties.

The Eastern and Northern Shoshones have received millions of dollars for their lost land. The U.S. government has also offered the Western Shoshones a cash settlement. Many do not want to accept the offer, however. To some Shoshones, there is not enough money in the world to pay for their lands. They vow to continue fighting until their homeland is returned to them.

The sun sets over the territory near the Shoshone-Bannock reservation at Fort Hall, Idaho.

THE WINNOWING TRAY GAME

Among Western Shoshone women, a favorite game was the winnowing tray game. Winnowing trays (*below*) were large shallow baskets the Shoshones used to harvest pine nuts. To play the game, Shoshone women placed wooden sticks into a tray. The sticks were painted red on one side. Players took turns shaking the tray. They won points by making the red side of the sticks land upright.

You can play a version of the winnowing tray game with Popsicle sticks and a basket.

WHAT YOU NEED:

12 Popsicle sticks
red paint
paint brush
basket at least 12 inches (30 centimeters) wide

WHAT TO DO:

1. Paint one side of each stick red and allow the paint to dry. Place the sticks in the basket.

2. Sit in a circle with the other players. Hand the basket of sticks to the first player. The first player should shake it so that the sticks fly into the air and then land back in the basket.

3. Count the number of sticks that land in the basket with their red side up. If the number is one, two, or five, the player should receive that many points and get another turn. If there is another number of red sides showing, the basket should be passed to the next player.

4. Continue the game until one player has twenty-five points.

PLACES TO VISIT

Eastern Shoshone Tribal Cultural Center
Fort Washakie, Wyoming
(307) 332-9106
http://www.wyshs.org/mus-shoshone.htm
The center displays photographs, treaties, maps, and other objects
dealing with Shoshone history.

National Museum of the American Indian
Washington, DC
(202) 633-1000
http://www.nmai.si.edu
This museum features exhibits about the Shoshones and other
American Indian tribes.

Sacajawea State Park
Pasco, Washington
(509) 545-2361
http://www.parks.wa.gov/parkpage.asp?selectedpark=Sacajawea
At this day park, visitors can follow the path of the Lewis and Clark
Expedition where the Columbia and Snake rivers meet. The park also
features the Sacajawea Interpretive Center.

Shoshone-Bannock Tribal Museum
Fort Hall, Idaho
(208) 237-9791
http://www.blacksmithinn.com/forthall.html
This museum includes photographs and information about the
Shoshone-Bannock tribes.

GLOSSARY

band: a group of American Indians who live and travel together. A band is usually part of a larger group, such as a tribe.

expedition: a group of people traveling together on a journey

Great Plains: a large grassy area in central North America that stretches thousands of miles from Canada to Texas

Pia Sokopia: the Shoshones' name for their homeland, meaning "Earth Mother"

piñon tree: a type of pine tree with nutlike seeds

rendezvous: an annual gathering of American Indian and non-native traders held in the American West during the early 1800s

reservation: an area of land set aside by the U.S. government for a particular American Indian group

Round Dance: a traditional Shoshone ceremony in which participants dance in a circle and sing songs

territory: an area of land

tipi: a cone-shaped home made of tall wooden poles and covered with animal skins

treaty: a written agreement between two or more nations or groups

tribal council: a group of people from different bands who are elected to make decisions for their reservation

tribe: a group of related American Indians who share the same language, customs, and religious beliefs

vision quest: a ceremony conducted by Indian youths, during which they waited for visions of spirits who would become their guides in life

FURTHER READING

Carter, Alden R. *The Shoshonis.* New York: Franklin Watts, 1989. This book is a useful introduction to Shoshone culture and history.

Erdrich, Lise. *Sacagawea.* Minneapolis: Carolrhoda Books, 2003. This biography tells the story of Sacagawea and her efforts to help the explorers Lewis and Clark.

Morris, Ann. *Grandma Maxine Remembers: A Native American Family Story.* Brookfield, CT: Millbrook Press, 2002. The author describes the lives of an eight-year-old Shoshone girl and her grandmother.

Washakie, John. *Yuse, the Bully and the Bear.* Fort Washakie, WY: Painted Pony, 2004. The great-grandson of Washakie shares this traditional Shoshone story of a boy who overcomes a bully. Glossary terms and illustration captions are in the Shoshone language.

WEBSITES

Eastern Shoshone Tribe
http://www.easternshoshone.net
This website offers information about events and businesses on the Wind River Indian Reservation.

Sho-Ban News Online
http://www.shobannews.com
News of the Shoshone-Bannock and other tribes can be found on this site.

Shoshone-Bannock Tribes
http://www.shoshonebannocktribes.com
The Shoshone-Bannock's official site presents their history in words and pictures.

Western Shoshone Defense Project
http://www.wsdp.org
This is the official site of the Western Shoshone Defense Project, an organization that wants Western Shoshones to get back their old homeland.

SELECTED BIBLIOGRAPHY

Crum, Steven J. *The Road on Which We Came (Po'i Pentun Tammen Kimmappeh): A History of the Western Shoshone.* Salt Lake City: University of Utah Press, 1994.

D'Azevedo, Warren L., ed. *Handbook of North American Indians: Great Basin.* Vol. 11. Washington, DC: Smithsonian Institution, 1986.

Dramer, Kim. *The Shoshone.* Philadelphia: Chelsea House Publishers, 1997.

Hoxie, Frederick E., ed. *Encyclopedia of North American Indians.* Boston: Houghton Mifflin, 1996.

Stamm, Henry E. *People of the Wind River: The Eastern Shoshones, 1825–1900.* Norman, OK: University of Oklahoma Press, 1999.

INDEX